D1242447

AWESOME DOGS

Saint Bernards

by Nathan Sommer

BELLWETHER MEDIA • MINNEAPOLIS, MN

Note to Librarians, Teachers, and Parents:

Blastoff! Readers are carefully developed by literacy experts and combine standards-based content with developmentally appropriate text.

Level 1 provides the most support through repetition of high-frequency words, light text, predictable sentence patterns, and strong visual support.

Level 2 offers early readers a bit more challenge through varied simple sentences, increased text load, and less repetition of high-frequency words.

Level 3 advances early-fluent readers toward fluency through increased text and concept load, less reliance on visuals, longer sentences, and more literary language.

Level 4 builds reading stamina by providing more text per page, increased use of punctuation, greater variation in sentence patterns, and increasingly challenging vocabulary.

Level 5 encourages children to move from "learning to read" to "reading to learn" by providing even more text, varied writing styles, and less familiar topics.

Whichever book is right for your reader, Blastoff! Readers are the perfect books to build confidence and encourage a love of reading that will last a lifetime!

This edition first published in 2018 by Bellwether Media, Inc.

No part of this publication may be reproduced in whole or in part without written permission of the publisher. For information regarding permission, write to Bellwether Media, Inc., Attention: Permissions Department, 5357 Penn Avenue South, Minneapolis, MN 55419.

Library of Congress Cataloging-in-Publication Data

Names: Sommer, Nathan, author.
Title: Saint Bernards / by Nathan Sommer.
Description: Minneapolis, MN : Bellwether Media, Inc., [2018] | Series:
   Blastoff! Readers. Awesome Dogs | Audience: Age 5-8. | Audience: K to
   grade 3. | Includes bibliographical references and index.
Identifiers: LCCN 2016052720 (print) | LCCN 2017013856 (ebook) | ISBN
   9781626176157 (hardcover : alk. paper) | ISBN 9781681033457 (ebook)
Subjects: LCSH: Saint Bernard dog–Juvenile literature.
Classification: LCC SF429.S3 (ebook) | LCC SF429.S3 S66 2018 (print) | DDC
   636.73–dc23
LC record available at https://lccn.loc.gov/2016052720

Editor: Betsy Rathburn   Designer: Kathy Petelinsek

Printed in the United States of America, North Mankato, MN.

Table of Contents

What Are Saint Bernards?

Saint Bernards are a huge, friendly dog **breed**. These gentle dogs make great family pets.

They love to make their
owners happy!

Saint Bernards have strong bodies. They can weigh up to 180 pounds (82 kilograms).

Saint Bernard Profile

wrinkled forehead

short muzzle

droopy cheeks

Life Span: 7 to 12 years

Trainability:

| 1 | 2 | 3 | 4 | 5 | 6 |

Hardest to train   Easiest to train

The **American Kennel Club** puts them in its **Working Group**.

Droopy Cheeks and Floppy Ears

Saint Bernards have big heads with short **muzzles**. They have **wrinkled** foreheads and **droopy** cheeks.

muzzle

Their floppy ears look
like rounded triangles.

Saint Bernards have short or long **coats**. These come in shades of brown and red.

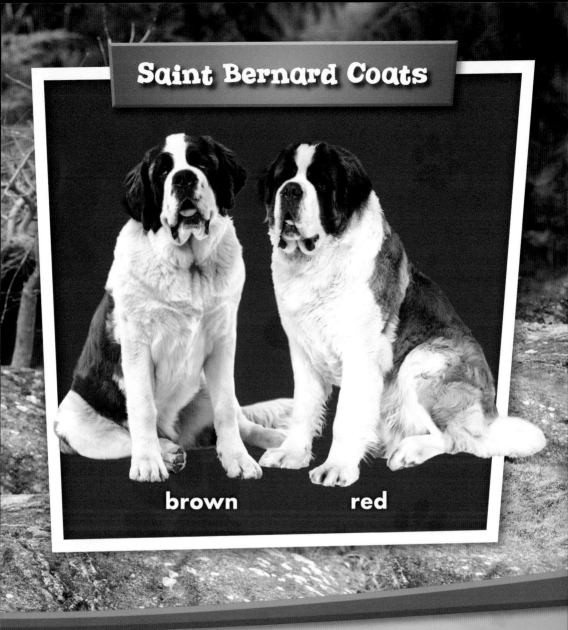

Saint Bernard Coats

brown   red

White markings appear on their chests, necks, and muzzles.

History of Saint Bernards

Saint Bernards have been around for **centuries**. They first began in Switzerland.

Switzerland

N W E S

Great Saint
Bernard Pass

Their name comes from the
Great Saint Bernard **Pass**.

At the pass, the dogs helped **monks** guard a **hospice**. They also helped rescue lost travelers.

Saint Bernards saved more than 2,000 people during that time!

By the 1800s, Saint Bernards were well known in the United States.

They soon became one of the
country's top breeds.

Saint Bernards are **loyal** dogs. They want to please their owners.

They are hard workers. Some even compete in weight-pulling events!

weight-pulling event

Saint Bernards are lovable
animals. They like to play with
other pets and children.

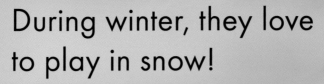

During winter, they love
to play in snow!

Glossary

American Kennel Club—an organization that keeps track of dog breeds in the United States

breed—a type of dog

centuries—hundreds of years

coats—the hair or fur covering some animals

droopy—saggy and hanging down

hospice—a hotel for travelers

loyal—having constant support for someone

monks—men who live apart from other people because of religious beliefs; monks have many rules that they must follow.

muzzles—the noses and mouths of some animals

pass—a path between two mountains

Working Group—a group of dog breeds that have a history of performing jobs for people

wrinkled—folded or creased

To Learn More

AT THE LIBRARY

Clapper, Nikki Bruno. *Saint Bernards*. North Mankato, Minn.: Capstone Press, 2016.

Nelson, Maria. *Saint Bernards*. New York, N.Y.: Gareth Stevens Pub., 2012.

Rudolph, Jessica. *Saint Bernard: Mountain Rescuer*. New York, N.Y.: Bearport Pub., 2012.

ON THE WEB

Learning more about Saint Bernards is as easy as 1, 2, 3.

1. Go to www.factsurfer.com.

2. Enter "Saint Bernards" into the search box.

3. Click the "Surf" button and you will see a list of related web sites.

With factsurfer.com, finding more information is just a click away.

Index

The images in this book are reproduced through the courtesy of: Sparkling Moments Photography, front cover; Grigorita Ko, pp. 4, 6, 11 (right), 12, 14, 16, 20; CSP_billylovesaj/ Age Fotostock, p. 5; cynoclub, p. 7; Aneta Jungerova, p. 8; David Pegzlz, pp. 8-9; Artush, pp. 10-11; Eric Isselee, p. 11 (left); MONTICO Lionel/ HEMIS.fr/ SuperStock, p. 13; URS FLUEELER/ EPA/ Nescom, p. 15; Becky Swora, p. 17; THEPALMER, p. 18; Anchorage Daily News/ Getty Images, p. 19; fotofrankyat, 21.